Population Perils

EDITORS

George W. Forell

William H. Lazareth

JUSTICE

BOOKS

FORTRESS PRESS   PHILADELPHIA

COPYRIGHT © 1979 BY FORTRESS PRESS

Library of Congress Cataloging in Publication Data

Main entry under title:
Population perils.
   (Justice books)
   Bibliography: p.
   1. Population—Moral and religious aspects—
Addresses, essays, lectures. 2. Population policy
—Moral and religious aspects—Addresses, essays,
lectures. I. Forell, George Wolfgang.
II. Lazareth, William Henry, 1928-   III. Series.
HQ766.2.P66   301.32   78-54548
ISBN 0-8006-1554-9

7118H78   Printed in the United States of America   1-1554

Contents

Regular contributors to Justice Books, in addition to the editors, include Elizabeth A. Bettenhausen, George H. Brand, John A. Evenson, Foster R. McCurley, Richard J. Niebanck, and John H. Reumann.

Population:
The World's Dilemma

Paul E. Lutz *

THE world's population is growing at a fantastic rate. This is a familiar statement we all have heard before—and sometime society must do something about the problem of too many people. But let no one be deceived—that sometime is today and solutions to the enormously complex population problems must be found immediately.

There are many who feel that the time for a solution came, in fact, decades ago. A golden opportunity was missed to solve this planet's most vexing problem. As our society is forced to confront the basic issues of population increase, profoundly complicated moral, ethical, theological, and humanitarian issues come rushing to the forefront. The population explosion is real—the problems we were told were to occur tomorrow are upon us today.

Is it necessarily bad that the current world's population is over 4.3 billion persons? Do we already have too many persons or can our planet adequately support 10 or 25 billion? It is my contention that a population much in excess of 4 billion cannot be sustained adequately now or in the future.

If we use an economic standard of the middle-class American, there is good evidence that the planet could support no more than 1.5 billion people at that level. Middle-class America may be a

*The author is Professor of Biology at the University of North Carolina (Greensboro).

poor standard to use; nonetheless, it does serve as a dramatic point of reference. If all the resources were equitably distributed to the 4.3 billion persons living today, each would be living on about 1/3 of the resources of an average American. The median household income for Americans in 1976 was $12,158, and 1/3 of this would be $4,053. Since the median household size is 2.89, this would mean an annual per capita income of only about $1,400. Such an economic level would leave everyone well below the poverty level currently defined by the U.S. government.

People put demands upon a multitude of resources that are present in finite, limited amounts. More people require more space, housing, food, energy, medicines and medical services, mineral resources, water, clean air, schools, churches, transportation, etc. Because natural resources are present in limited amounts, more people simply put more stresses on these vital, life-sustaining commodities. Environmental issues such as energy, resource depletion, land use, and pollution are inexorably tied to population. Absolute solutions to these related problems will not be found until the issues of population growth are realized and understood.

There are honest differences in opinion as to the maximum number of persons that can be supported globally; but whatever these global limits are, they either have been or shortly will be exceeded. Therefore, society should be deeply concerned about the rate the population is growing.

The growth rate is determined by the difference between the birth and death rates—both of which are usually expressed as numbers (born or died) per 1,000 people per year. For example, according to the Environmental Fund, the world birth rate in 1976–77 was 34 per 1,000 population and the death rate was 13 per 1,000. Subtracting mortality from fertility provides a growth rate of 21 per 1,000 which, when converted to a percentage figure, becomes 2.1% per year. While an annual growth rate of 2.1% is a much lower rate than the interest rate most financial institutions are paying currently, such a comparison is very deceptive. In terms of population growth, 2.1% is an heretofore unheard of rate. Never before has the human population growth rate been so high.

A growth rate of 2.1% means that the population size will double about every 33 years. If this rate of increase is sustained, in 33 years the population size will be 8.6 billion, in 33 more years (in the year 2044) there will be 17.2 billion, and in 100 years (2078) the population size would be 34.4 billion or eight times the current size.

Population growth is described as being exponential or logarithmic. A quantity doubling repeatedly will produce an astronomical number in a surprisingly short period of time. Arithmetical increase proceeds: $1 \rightarrow 2 \rightarrow 3 \rightarrow 4 \rightarrow 5$, while exponential increase proceeds: $1 \rightarrow 2 \rightarrow 4 \rightarrow 8 \rightarrow 16$. Moreover, such exponential growth is not immediately evident to the casual observer until it has reached almost massive proportions.

To illustrate the phenomenon of exponential growth, there is a story of a young man who proposed to an employer that he would work for him for 30 days; further, he proposed that his salary for the first day would be only 1 penny if his salary would double for each of the succeeding 29 days. His salary, therefore, was $0.01, 0.02, 0.04, 0.08, 0.16, 0.32, and 0.64 for the first seven days, respectively. His salary for day 10 was $5.12, for day 15 was $163.84, for day 20 was $5,242.88, and for day 25 was $167,772.16. On day 30 (had the employer been able even to stay in business) his salary for that day would have been $5,368,709.12, and his total earnings for the 30-day period would have exceeded 10.5 million dollars! The point of this story is that repeated doubling, even of a small, initial amount, will result in unbelievable numbers within a short span of time.

Because of exponential growth, the world's population size will, in the near future, be expanding at an incomprehensible rate. At the current rate of increase, 90 million more births than deaths occur each year. That is a staggering figure when one considers that 90 million more persons each year are equivalent, for example, to (1) the entire population of Nigeria or Bangladesh, or (2) the population of the United Kingdom, Scandinavia, and Belgium combined, or (3) 40% of the U.S. population. Certainly then, one of the most insidious population problems is that of rate of increase.

THE PAST TRENDS

Historically, the population explosion is quite a recent deviation from a long-established pattern of very slow growth. Over the millennia the human population probably never increased more than 0.1% per year until the late seventeenth century. This low growth rate during the first million or so years of the human species was a reflection of the death rate almost keeping pace with the birth rate. In the last half of the seventeenth century, a number of trends were initiated that resulted eventually in a higher future growth rate. Migration into the New World and the beginnings of remarkable breakthroughs in many health-related areas were to reduce mortality substantially. While the birth rate has decreased since 1750, the death rate, especially that for infants, has dropped precipitously.

Since 1750 growth rates have steadily increased as can be seen from Table 1. Perhaps the most important data are to be found in

TABLE 1
GLOBAL POPULATION INCREASES
Population Size (Millions)
During the Period at the

Period	Beginning	End	Growth Rate (%)
A.D. 1–1750	300	800	0.05
1750–1800	800	1,000	0.44
1800–1850	1,000	1,300	0.52
1850–1900	1,300	1,700	0.54
1900–1950	1,700	2,500	0.79
1950–1975	2,500	4,000	1.71
1975–2000	4,000	ca. 7,000	2.10

the growth rate column. Not only are there more persons in more recent periods, but the growth rate has also increased. In the first 1750 years after the time of Christ, the population doubled about every 1,200 years. At the present growth rate, the population will double about every 33 years. These figures suggest a truly remarkable increase in the way in which the growth rate is itself increasing. Such an escalating rate enormously compounds the phenomenon of exponential growth. This increase in the growth rate is, in effect, the same as giving the hypothetical young employee an *extra daily raise progressively earlier in each day!*

THE PRESENT SITUATION

Table 2 presents some relevant demographic data for the major world regions in mid-1977; this information shows that population data are not the same throughout the world.

TABLE 2
POPULATION ESTIMATES, MID-1977[1]

	Population Estimates (Millions)	Growth Rate (%)	Birth Rate (per 1,000 Population)	Death Rate (per 1,000 Population)	1950 Population (Millions)	Increase from 1950 to 1977 (%)
World	4,307.4	2.1	34	13	2,542.8	69
Africa	451.2	2.8	46	20	218.9	106
Asia	2,505.7	2.4	38	14	1,408.5	78
North America	247.3	0.8	14	9	166.1	49
Canada	23.4	1.3	16	7	13.7	71
U.S.A.	223.9	0.8	14	9	152.3	47
Latin America	341.8	2.8	37	9	164.4	108
Europe	478.8	0.6	15	11	392.4	22
U.S.S.R.	259.4	1.0	18	9	180.1	44
Oceania	21.8	1.8	22	9	12.4	76

1. The Environmental Fund World Population Estimates, 1977. Data for tables used by permission of the Environmental Fund.

Some areas have dramatically different patterns as exemplified by the two Americas. Both North America and Latin America had similar-sized populations in 1950. Since 1950 there are 49%

more North Americans but 108% more Latin Americans. The death rates are the same for both, but the fertility rate for Latin America is more than 2½ times that for North America. As a result the growth rate in North America is 0.8% per year, and at this rate it will take about 80 years for the population to double in size. Yet, in Latin America the growth rate is 2.8% per year, and the population size will double every 24 years. What has happened in the two Americas to produce such dramatically divergent trends? The answer in part lies in a phenomenon called demographic transition.

The historical process of the demographic transition is preceded by a long history of high birth and high death rates. The transition begins with a decline in the death rate achieved by increasing and improving health care, hygiene, public health measures, improving diets, and by reducing the incidence of debilitating diseases. As health care improves there is a concomitant improvement in the general economic conditions. Industrialization, mechanization and improved standards of living take place. Per capita incomes increase, and many services (e.g., insurance, social security, retirement) become available. Persons no longer rely entirely on their present or future children to care for them in sickness or in their old age. Thus, one important reason for having large numbers of children is removed. As a result of these and many other factors, the birth rate usually drops within a few decades after the decrease in mortality. With a low birth rate and a low death rate, a relatively stable population size is achieved.

In North America the demographic transition was virtually complete by the middle of this century as it was in most other developed countries (DCs) including those in Europe, Scandinavia, and the U.S.S.R. These countries have relatively stable populations with low birth and death rates.

Yet in Latin America as well as in other less developed countries (LDCs) in Africa and Asia, there is little evidence that the demographic transition has occurred, or that it will be completed in the foreseeable future. Death rates fell dramatically during the middle decades of this century, but fertility rates have remained high or have fallen little in the LDCs. The momentum of population growth in many of the LDCs is apparently too strong to stop via the lowering of birth rates alone. Rather, many people predict a decline in population in the LDCs caused by higher death rates.

Many positive things have happened for people in developed countries leading to a better and longer life. The awful scourges of deadly contagious diseases are over. Instead of dying early in life, persons in the DCs now survive to their sixties and seventies, and do so in relative comfort. We enjoy many of the advantages that have accrued as a result of revolutions in medicine, agriculture, science, and technology. Life in the affluent countries is truly much better than it ever has been before—much better than our ancestors could ever have dreamed was possible.

In stark contrast to the conditions found in the developed nations, there has emerged a grim dilemma for about 2/3 of the global population. At least 90% of the annual world population increase occurs in the lesser developed countries. These countries already have a much lower standard of living and can ill-afford the pressures of additional population.

It is precisely in the LDCs where food shortages are the most critical and where there is little hope of improving crop yields. There is little money to purchase mechanized or irrigation equipment, fertilizers, or essential fuel for machines which could enhance productivity. Health care in many LDCs is often lacking with few doctors to help alleviate the suffering, illnesses, and diseases of the masses. Life expectancy is low and mortality is high. A new child born in most LDCs in 1978 has very little to look forward to except suffering, hunger, disease, an early death, and little chance of ever changing these conditions. The gap between the DCs and the LDCs grows wider with the passage of time.

THE FUTURE

The most fundamental problem in the LDCs in the future will be the production of enough food for the large and rapidly expanding population. Conversely, the most important concern in the DCs will be how to control and wisely use the world's limited natural resources.

Both problems are intimately related—first to the vital struggle of the LDCs to raise their standard of living, and secondly for the DCs to sustain their high standard of living. Can the developed world continue its excessively affluent lifestyle involving the consumption and wastage of precious natural resources at the expense of the lives of people in the LDCs? Can the LDCs continue to experience rapid population increase when there is no immediate way to increase food production accordingly?

Food is the primary issue as expanding populations demand more of the world's resources. Food production has kept pace with population growth up until the last several decades. Shortly after it was generally realized that shortfalls in food production were occurring, the Green Revolution arrived. Dramatic agricultural breakthroughs involved the development of new hybrid strains of wheat and rice that doubled or tripled production over former yields. The effects of the Green Revolution were magnified by a number of fortuitous, related events including exceptionally good weather for grain crops. In the 1970s, however, poor weather and still more mouths to feed have more than negated the benefits of the Green Revolution.

Currently, the population growth is surpassing the increase in food production resulting in, quite simply, progressively more hungry people. Food production can be increased to some degree in many parts of the world by utilizing higher producing strains of grain, converting more land into arable use, using more intensive cultivation practices, instituting land reform measures, employing modern equipment, and massive use of fertilizers and irrigation techniques. But no single one or any combination of these changes will be a panacea for the world's hungry people, and they can even eventually be counterproductive.

For example, extensive use of fertilizer promotes better yields for a time; yet fertilizer leaves behind toxic minerals and high-yielding crops tend to deplete other minerals so that the soil simply "wears out" and productivity diminishes. Conversion of tropical rain forests into crop lands invariably is very inefficient since such areas grow fantastic forests but very poor food crops. Massive use of fertilizer or continued irrigation can result in severe ecological damage not only to the immediate area but to surrounding habitats as well.

The effects of diminishing natural resources, especia
fuels, will also offset most agricultural advances. Th
situation: food production cannot keep pace with a pc
growing at 2.1% per annum. Either the rate of increase of
population size must be lowered substantially or we can expect
much more hunger and a much higher mortality rate in the
LDCs.

POPULATION REGULATION

Population size for a given area or country is regulated by three
variables: fertility, mortality, and migration. A growing
population can be converted into one with zero growth by (1)
reducing fertility, (2) out-migration, and (3) increasing mortality. Fertility has dropped dramatically in the DCs and to a
lesser extent in some LDCs. Enhanced fertility is undoubtedly a
reflection of many component factors, but it seems to be in-
versely correlated with levels of income—the poorer the family or
country, the higher the birth rate.

Historically, an expanding population could remain stable in
size by migration of part of the population into other regions.
International migrations were especially prevalent in the last
three centuries and were an effective mechanism for distributing
excess persons into vast, sparsely settled regions. Such migrations
continue today even though the world no longer has inhabitable,
low density space. Such migrations can be expected to increase
from the LDCs as excess population pressures force persons to try
to escape the deteriorating situations in their own countries. Such
migrants to the DCs will represent the more affluent and the
better educated of the LDCs; thus, the gap between the LDCs
and the DCs will be even further widened.

Internal or intranational migrations continue at present as
persons move between rural and urban areas. In recent years
there has been a tendency for the affluent to move away from
cities into surrounding suburban areas or rural countryside and
the poor into the inner cities. This produces an inner city mainly
populated with the poor, minority persons, and the poorly
educated—creating, in effect, a grouping similar to the
population of a LDC. In North America today, microcosms have

been established of "lesser developed peoples" interspersed with "developed people." The social and political problems that exist today in the U.S. and Canada are but a small sample of the situation for most of the rest of the world.

Mortality has been a most important mechanism in population control throughout our existence. Famines, epidemics, plagues, and other natural events along with wars have been instrumental in keeping the mortality rate high and population increase minimal. But in the last three centuries, the effects of most diseases have been reduced, especially in children. Death has now been effectively delayed until the post-reproductive period. Thus, a greater percentage of the population now reaches reproductive age and this certainly enhances the growth rate.

How then are solutions to the problems of population growth to be developed? What are the best methods to achieve a stable population size? In simplistic terms, the population of a country or region can be regulated by fertility and/or mortality.

Reducing fertility is obviously the most sensible method for stabilizing population size. There is a close correlation between the level of development of a country, its birth rate, and the use of contraceptives. The DCs all have low birth rates and high contraceptive use, while the LDCs have much higher fertility rates and much lower use of contraceptives. Birth control and family planning measures are now being practiced in countries having about 70% of the world's population, but their effect to date is a matter of conjecture.

It is interesting to note that demographic transitions were carried out in both Europe and North America without the benefit of either birth control measures or family planning programs. Economic changes, rather than family planning programs alone, were clearly responsible for the substantial alteration of fertility rates.

It is imperative that humanity slow the escalating population growth by reducing fertility. If this cannot be achieved, then the inevitable result will be a rise in the mortality rate. This is obviously not the best or even a desirable means, but it is one way to achieve a stable population. Mortality will probably be increased not only by the lack of medical and paramedical services, but by the lack of food. Hunger stalks more than half of the world's population every day, and starvation is a very effective factor in increasing mortality.

Can we rationally and sanely solve the problems of the population explosion by controlling fertility, or will we, by default, let nature solve our problems for us impersonally and rigidly but very effectively by hunger and famine? Zero population growth will be achieved in the future by one of these two methods!

SOME VEXING QUESTIONS

Other writers in this volume will give considerable attention to the critical ethical and humanitarian dimensions associated with population growth. Yet I want to pose briefly some vexing questions. The population explosion with all of its by-products generates numerous ethical problems. For many questions there appear to be no right answers and many wrong ones. Because the population problems are so enormous and global in dimension, even partial solutions will be extraordinarily difficult.

One whole group of solutions has been proposed recently and goes under the title of "lifeboat ethics" (Hardin, G. "Living on a Lifeboat," *BioScience* 24, (1974), pp. 561–568). Metaphorically, each rich nation amounts to a lifeboat almost full of relatively rich people. The poor of the world are in many other, much more crowded lifeboats. Continuously, some of the poor fall (or are pushed) out of their overly crowded craft into the water. They swim for a time and eventually insist that they be pulled aboard one of the rich lifeboats. The central question in lifeboat ethics involves what the passengers on the rich lifeboat are to do.

Suppose we imagine we are on an American lifeboat with a capacity of sixty and there are fifty people on board. Imagine 1,000 persons swimming in the water near our boat begging for assistance. What do we do? There are three basic alternatives: (1) admit no one else to the boat and thus provide us with a "safety factor" in the event one is needed; (2) admit only ten more to bring our boat up to full capacity and let the remaining 990 drown; or (3) respond by being our brothers' and sisters' keeper, take all the needy into our lifeboat which is now swamped, and everyone drowns.

The lifeboat metaphor is a useful one even if it oversimplifies the situation. Some very fundamental decisions will necessarily be made in the near future by individuals or governments in North America that will affect the entire world. What are we in the DCs to do about the LDCs?

Alternative 1. We admit no one else to our lifeboat. This means we turn our backs on most of the rest of the world and let them solve their own problems or perish. We let each country achieve zero population growth by reducing fertility or increasing mortality. The DCs do nothing to help or hinder the local decision. We send them no food, no assistance of any sort—they are left to make it on their own.

Alternative 2. We provide assistance to a few of the many needy by bringing them aboard our lifeboat. They will share equally with us, but the masses left behind will get nothing. Do we make the decision on which ten to help based on their natural resources, their being strategic to our defense, their government's similarity to ours, their skin color or nationality, their historical similarities to us? What bases do we use? Are there enough Solomons among us to exert the necessary wisdom to make such life-and-death decisions?

Alternative 3. We extend the hand of humanitarianism to everyone. We help them aboard by being of whatever assistance we can. We share fully our resources with the full realization that those we keep alive will, in turn, continue to be a factor in sustaining a high rate of population increase. We share our wealth, our food, our resources with the LDCs and let the LDCs share their people with us. Our lifeboat is swamped, and eventually it sinks and we all perish.

We in North America and in the other DCs can make it if we follow Alternatives 1 or 2. We can survive physically—but we doubtless will die spiritually because of our greed and selfishness in not helping all those in need. Nothing can be worse for us than to die spiritually. We must solve the problems of population. Our time has almost run out; the clock is about to strike midnight, and our world will turn into a pumpkin in a moment.

Historical Disasters and Final Judgment (Series A, B)

Foster R. McCurley and John H. Reumann *

OVERPOPULATION was scarcely a problem in the biblical world, or for antiquity in general. Rather the goal often was to have large families for economic and other reasons. But famine and hunger were a constant threat. The lectionary preacher therefore has only limited opportunity, especially in the closing weeks of the A cycle and the beginning of the B series of readings, to deal directly with "the world's dilemma," but some texts do lend themselves to getting into the current challenge of "population."

POPULATION IN ANTIQUITY

For ancient Israel, amid war, disease, and natural calamities in a basically agricultural society, the need was for many children with a high preference for males. (Recall the papyrus letter from Hilarion to Alia, "If by chance you bear a child, if it is a boy, let it be; if it is a girl, cast it out." Contrast the *Epistle to Diognetus* 5.6, Christians "do not abandon the babies that are born.")

Indeed it is this situation which deserves serious consideration for understanding the statement in the Priestly account of creation: "Be fruitful and multiply" (Gen. 1:28; also 1:22 in reference to animal life). In the first place, the literary context

*The authors serve as Professors of Old and New Testaments at the Lutheran Theological Seminary at Philadelphia.

helps us understand the imperatives as blessings rather than as commands. The statement is prefaced in 1:28 by "And God blessed them, and God said to them. . . ." At 1:22 the introduction is even more explicit: "And God blessed them, saying. . . ."

In the second place, the historical context of the writing of this material is crucial here. The Priestly writer addressed landless, hopeless exiles in the land of Babylon in the sixth century B.C. For him and his audience the "fruitful and multiply" formula proclaimed the continued power of God and his blessing in an apparently God-forsaken situation (see also Jeremiah's letter to the exiles at Jer. 29:4–14, esp. v. 6).

Recently it has been pointed out that the formula is also concerned with the possession of land—that it points toward a future when the land would be restored to the Israelites and fertility celebrated (see W. Brueggemann and H. W. Wolff, *The Vitality of Old Testament Traditions*, pp. 101-113). In this and similar writings there is evident a view that the purpose of marriage is procreation. Josephus wrote, "No sexual intercourse except that of husband and wife, and that only for the procreation of children" (*Against Apron* 2.199). Thus in a precise way the Priestly theologian addressed the needs of his audience.

APOCALYPTIC POSSIBILITIES

What if the human situation is changed so that the blessings given to the woman and man created in God's image might mean *reducing* the birth rate in order that each person could live a level of life that God intends? Although biblical writers were not confronted with situations where the avoidance of procreation or limiting of populations was called for, this is the challenge that confronts us in modern times.

In the first century of the church, those who were convinced of an impending apocalypse urged the avoidance of marriage and the bearing of children. The Essenes were said by Josephus to have disdained marriage, though they adopted the children of others (*War* 2.120). They had no slaves because injustice would be involved, nor wives because "dissension" would be introduced

(*Ant.* 18.21; cf. Prov. 25:24). The references in the Dead Sea Scrolls themselves suggest that practices varied from time to time, sometimes assuming celibacy and other times recognizing marriage (1QSa 1.8–9).

"Eschatological celibacy" has been appealed to as an explanation for the situation behind 1 Corinthians 7:1–7. There Paul suggests that husband and wife may by mutual consent, for a time, deny themselves to each other sexually in order to devote themselves to prayer. There is no cultic asceticism here (as in the Greek world), nor any notion that celibacy is a higher state (as with the Cynics), but that simply "because of the times," including "the impending distress" (7:26), one may wish to forgo marriage or be ruled by the charisma of abstinence (cf. 7:7).

Paul has other grounds as well for suggesting celibacy, such as the possibility of undivided attention to the work of the Lord (7:32–34). But Paul is in basic agreement with the apocalyptic tradition which says, "Alas for those who are with child . . . in those days" (Mark 13:17). How does one live responsibly when conditions change?

"Apocalyptic" is a word used by some to describe the current exponential increase of population on earth while resources are dwindling and food production is not keeping pace. In the Apocalypse of John, Death and Hades are preceded in the parade of the four horsemen by the black horse symbolizing famine, which comes after war (Rev. 6:1–8). Bread is rationed, and some commentators think the reference to the high price of barley and wheat reflects the position of John against a governmental policy which promoted luxuries but made basics expensive.

Might an apocalyptic understanding offer an avenue for broaching the population question today, without becoming a fundamentalistic alarmist or proof-texter? The epistles for the last Sundays of the church year are regularly apocalyptic in tone, in the A Series from 1 Thessalonians. On 23 Pentecost there is reference at 1 Thessalonians 1:10 to "the wrath to come," and while "the *orge*" has been variously interpreted as God's personal judgment to come on sin—rather than as an impersonal principle of cause and effect (so C. H. Dodd)--might it include the things leading up to the End which we mortals bring upon ourselves?

On 24 Pentecost we may read the epistle 1 Thessalonians
4:13–14 (15–18). It sketches an apocalyptic drama about "the
End" (including what sect groups have come to call "the Rap-
ture") which Paul employs to comfort (v. 18) the Thessalonians,
arm them with hope (v. 13), and undergird the ethic of getting
back to work responsibly (5:14). What might words of comfort,
admonition, hope, and responsible living in Paul's universal
perspectives mean for us today regarding population? The next
Sunday's lessons from 5:1–11 might be used in a similar way: how
are we to live, given "the times and seasons" *of our day*? The
excerpt from 1 Corinthians 15, vv. 20–28, on the Festival of Christ
the King, has possibilities for helping people think beyond the
present moment to the grand sweep of history.

FAMINE, A BIBLICAL REALITY

Literal starvation was a menace constantly haunting ancient
civilizations. "If the rains do not come, or the Nile overflow its
banks" was a perpetual worry and people lived from harvest to
harvest. In the Bible the dreaded reality of famine is attested
frequently and in some instances serves as the motivation for
migrations. Ruth's in-laws moved to Moab because of famine in
Judah (Ruth 1:1); Abraham left the Negeb for Egypt (Gen.
12:10), and apparently Isaac had contemplated the same (Gen.
26:1–2).

Of course, it is the Joseph story above all (Genesis 37–50) which
dramatizes the need for people in Canaan to head for Egypt when
famine struck (see chaps. 41ff.). The tradition of the seven years
of plenty followed by seven years of want is attested in Egyptian
literature as well. Even that land with its relatively consistent
overflowing Nile experienced periods of drought and famine.

There are two features of the Joseph story, however, which are
especially relevant to the issue of famine. First, the Egyptian
Pharaoh is portrayed as a humanitarian who offers freely "the fat
of the land" to Joseph's entire family living in famine-struck
Canaan (Gen. 45:16ff. and 47:1ff.). Interestingly, an Egyptian
text addressed to Pharaoh called "the Report of a Frontier Official" indicates that a state official on the eastern end of Egypt

allowed the passage of Bedouin tribes of Edom into Egypt "to keep them alive and to keep their cattle alive." That a copy of this letter was found among a group of exercises for school children demonstrates that such charitable descriptions of the Pharaoh were taught as part of Egypt's educational process. Perhaps coincidentally—but nevertheless interestingly—this view of the Pharaoh and of "the Egyptian lifeboat" corresponds with the portrayal in the biblical story of Joseph. What a positive image for one who is not of the chosen Israelite race!—or of the Christian church!

Second, however, the real hero of the Joseph story is God. As Joseph explains to his brothers, "God sent me before you to preserve for you a remnant on earth and to keep alive for you many survivors" (Gen. 45:7; 7 Epiphany C). And again at the end of the story, Joseph puts it like this: "As for you, you meant it for evil against me; but God meant it for good, to bring it about that many people should be kept alive, as they are today" (Gen. 50:20; 17 Pentecost A). Thus it is God who uses other people and their wisdom in times of famine in order to do his work of caring for the hungry (see Job 5:20).

Famine, as evidenced in these biblical texts (see also 2 Sam. 21:1; Acts 11:28), is unfortunately as modern as the calamity which afflicted sub-Sahara Africa and Bangladesh in the early 1970s. Sometimes caused by lack of rains, famine occurs also from insect invasion (see Amos 4:9) and from human warfare (see Isa. 1:7; 3:1, 7). There are terrifying effects of what hunger will cause people to do—even cannibalism (see 2 Kings 6:25–30). None of these passages comes up in the lectionary, however.

INSIGHTS FROM THE PERICOPES

Among the pertinent texts which do appear in the lectionary is Isaiah 25:6–9 (21 Pentecost A). This passage is part of a separate unit in the Book of Isaiah; chapters 24–27 comprise what is called "the Apocalypse of Isaiah" and were written four to six centuries after the prophet Isaiah.

Such apocalyptic literature arises when times are bad—when persecution is rampant, when destruction seems inevitable, when hopes in history are dashed. Pessimism with regard to the writer's present situation is contrasted in dualistic fashion with an optimism regarding a new age. That new age would come with the sudden intervention of God on his day—a time when he would destroy evil and by his victory establish himself as king over the universe (see Isa. 24:21–23).

Thus apocalyptic pronouncements set forth contrasts to the present scene. This particular pericope looks forward to that day when the nations of the whole earth will feast together on Mt. Zion, when suffering and mourning will cease because there will be no death, and when the Lord's people will experience peace. Therefore, the present scene of the author was one of reproach, suffering, death, and hostility of nations. The great feast to take place when the Lord becomes king is primarily a banquet in which the nations are brought into fellowship with God.

Parallels to such a meal have been traced in various other cultures, including Canaanite Baalism and Persian Zoroastrianism. But at the same time such a feast might also represent a contrast to the present scene in which peoples the world over do not and cannot eat their fill. Thus the hunger of this world will also be reversed when God establishes his kingdom. Such a future meal in the kingdom is attested in New Testament passages, Matthew 8:11 and Luke 7:28; Matthew 22:1–10 and Luke 14:15–24; Mark 14:25 and parallels.

In order to avoid a purely apocalyptic outlook which pessimistically stresses such horrors as poverty, hunger, and disease— and in order to stress the "already but not yet" nature of God's kingdom—we must look at another pericope, Isaiah 61:1–3, 10–11 (3 Advent B). Here the anonymous prophet announces that he has been anointed "to bring good tidings to the afflicted; . . . to bind up the brokenhearted, to proclaim liberty to the captives, and the opening of the prison to those who are bound; to proclaim the year of the Lord's favor, and the day of vengeance of our God; to comfort all who mourn . . ." (vv. 1c–2).

The prophet here looks to the imminence of the Jubilee Year (see Lev. 25:10) which he identifies with the Day of the Lord and thus with his kingdom. The era of salvation is breaking forth, and the people can expect a change in their personal sufferings. Indeed, to herald that new condition the Lord has commissioned this particular person to announce victory (the specific meaning of Hebrew *bisser*) to the physically afflicted. (On the basis of the Greek word here, one could render "to evangelize to the afflicted.")

The releasing of the captives and the victory of the afflicted must be understood as relief for prisoners, the hungry, the naked, and the homeless (see Isa. 58:6-7). Caring for the likes of such folk is the business of God, who, as king over the world, sets in contrast what was and what will be (see Isa. 61:3). The pericopes end at verses 10-11 with an individual's psalm of praise and concludes with a confident expression that God will effect the blessings he has promised.

By no means unrelated to the concern of the previous pericope, Ezekiel 34:11-16, 23-24 (Christ the King A) attests to the actual and physical care of suffering people. The pericope begins immediately after God's indictment against those shepherds of Israel who have failed to strengthen the weak, heal the sick, bind up the crippled, bring back the strayed, and seek the lost (see v. 4). Those shepherds or rulers of Israel allowed the sheep (the people) to be scattered and to become food rather than to be fed.

Thus the Lord takes upon himself that old image of shepherd which kings from Mesopotamia to Israel applied to themselves; the true shepherd who will seek out his exiled people, bring them back to their own land, feed them, bind up the crippled among them, strengthen the weak, and care for them by a "pastor's pattern." "The fat sheep" who have benefited from the misfortunes of "the lean sheep" will experience God's separation, while the lean sheep will be saved (vv. 20-22). It's clear from this which of the "lifeboat options" God the king chooses for himself!

Further, God promises to set up his own shepherd—a Davidic prince who will feed the people and be their shepherd. The influence of this passage on Jesus' understanding of himself as the Good Shepherd (John 10) is unmistakable. Further the image leads R. H. Fuller to see the possibility for "a humanitarian message" here: "the loving service of the Christian church can thus be expounded as an expression of the Christly care as king and shepherd" (*Preaching the New Lectionary* [1974], p. 281).

Of a quite different nature from those pericopes is Leviticus 19:1-2, 15-18 (23 Pentecost A). These verses from the so-called Holiness Code (Leviticus 17-26) provide a few pieces of the priestly concern for responsible cultic and ethical behavior.

It has been argued that 19:13-18 constitute a Decalogue; in that case our pericope contains laws 6-10 of an original unit. These laws are concerned with justice in judgment, partiality, slandering and false witnessing, hate of neighbor, and vengeance. Each set or pair of laws is established by the authority of God himself: "I am the Lord." The final pair includes the overriding ethical principle: "You shall love your neighbor as yourself" immediately before the authoritative self-identification of the Lord. That principle, called by Jesus the second great commandment (Matt. 23:39), means that love of the self becomes the measure of behavior toward others. It assumes that one must identify the needs of others as well as one's own needs and that one can act in love to serve the other as oneself.

Pertinent to our concern for dealing with famine as a population problem are other verses in Leviticus 19 which are related to the "Love your neighbor" principle. Verses 9-10 instruct the people of God to leave in the field a portion of each harvest so that the poor and the sojourner have something to eat; again follows the formula, "I am the Lord your God." That same instruction is given in the list of humanitarian concerns in Deuteronomy 24; verses 19-21 command the reaper to leave food in the fields and on the trees for the sojourner, the fatherless, and the widow. The motive for such behavior is: "You shall remember that you were a slave in the land of Egypt; therefore I command you to do this" (v. 22). The "lifeboat option" is unmistakably clear—in Leviticus 19 on the basis of the authority of God and the love of neighbor, and in Deuteronomy 24 on the basis of redemption from slavery. The parallels for the Christian community are too obvious to belabor.

Matthew 5:1-12 (All Saints Sunday; 4 Epiphany A) sets forth the Beatitudes as a way to live which is reminiscent of the principle about loving the neighbor (Lev. 19:18). Jesus' teaching on the mountain raises the question of what being poor, meek, merciful, and a peacemaker might mean today in deciding about the "lifeboat ethic."

A topical sermon on how the early church responded to famine might be an interesting experiment, especially as a congregation seeks to support "Church World Service" or other hunger and advocacy programs with its financial gifts. Acts 11:27–30 and all the references to Paul's project of a collection for "the poor" in Jerusalem (Gal. 2:10; 1 Cor. 16:1–4; 2 Corinthians 8–9; e.g.) would be pertinent. However, one should also be aware that Paul's undertaking was viewed not merely as physical relief, but as a means of binding together two wings of the church, Jewish and Gentile, into a unity as a part of God's plan of salvation. Cf. J. Munck, *Paul and the Salvation of Mankind* (1959), pp. 286ff., or K. F. Nickle, *The Collection: A Study of Paul's Strategy* (SBT 48; 1966), esp. pp. 100–43. In our day, of course, we must go far beyond financial giving, of amounts large and small, to ask what Christian responsibility on planet Earth involves for all our fellow-humans.

LIFEBOAT ETHICS

The three alternatives sketched above (p. 15) for us on the "American lifeboat" pose the population problem starkly. Human pragmatism and the urge to survive push us towards (1) the isolationist answer of turning our back on the rest of the world or, at best, towards (2) selective charity. The challenge of the question, "Am I my brother's keeper?" (Gen. 4:9), coupled with the answer we know from the parable about the Good Samaritan (Luke 10:25–37) and the love of God which we have enjoyed call us to a more self–giving, self–effacing solution (3), or at least (2) a fuller sharing of what we have.

As noted above, the Beatitudes (especially Matt. 5:4–5, 7, 9) impel us to an answer which makes less of self and more of others. The texts mentioned from Genesis 4 and Luke 10 could be used to discuss the specific question of what we in North America shall do about problems of population as time runs out. At the least, an adjustment in lifestyle and living standards seems called for.

R. H. Fuller more pointedly suggests heeding the gospel for 20 Pentecost A with all its allegorical overtones. Matthew 21:33–43 is the story about the vineyard taken from the tenants to whom it had been entrusted by God and given to "other tenants who will give him the fruits in their seasons." Once directed against Israel (cf. also Isa. 5:1–7 and the use of Ps. 80:7–15), the parable is a threatening message to us about how we have exercised our stewardship as a church and as a people. The parable, according to Fuller, is "dynamite" against "the church in the Western world, with a threat that the leadership of the Christian cause will pass, say to Africans."

It is worth recalling that the question of population growth in relation to resources was introduced to the popular mind by a British clergyman, Thomas Robert Malthus, who first published his *Essay on the Principle of Population as it Affects the Future Improvement of Society* in 1798. It grew out of a debate with the optimistic views of his father, who, like others, in the age of revolution, looked toward the perfectability of society. The son combatted this view by asking whether the achievement of a happy society would not be precluded by miseries resulting from a population which increased faster than the food supply.

Malthus later taught history at the East India Company's College at Haileybury. It boggles the mind to think that the founder of "Malthusianism" trained bureaucrats to go to that most populous subcontinent where his theory hits with special poignancy. In spite of the much heralded Green Revolution in agriculture, the population of India, Pakistan, and Bangladesh continues to outstrip resources of the subcontinent. Malthus saw war, disease, and poverty as keeping population down, and after 1803 he added "moral restraint" as a necessary preventive check. Today, his question, with all its moral searchings for those in the "lifeboat," is upon the Western world.

THE SHEEP AND THE GOATS

While pertinent to the population question, because it asks what one did for the hungry, thirsty, naked, sick, and prisoners, the "parable" of the Sheep and the Goats (Matt. 25:31–46) has possibilities of application in many social-justice questions. (Tolstoy loved it, cf. "The Tale of the Shoemaker, Martin Avdejic.") In recent years it has become the parade example for preachers and even for those who do not find much use for the

Bible to inculcate concern for outcasts, for those who suffer from famine, and for all victims of injustice. It is a favorite text in the Theology of Liberation. Called "the Mount Everest of Synoptic criticism," waiting majestically to be scaled, it stands invitingly before the preacher on the last Sunday of the church year, chosen because Christ appears as king in the parable.

We may begin with the fact that it is not really a parable. The only comparison occurs in verses 33–34, the Son of man will separate the nations "as a shepherd separates the sheep from the goats," to the right and left respectively. That imagery, familiar from daily life in Jesus' day, also could reflect judgment by Yahweh as depicted in Ezekiel 34:17–31. Singular is the designation, however, of the Son of man as "king" (vv. 34, 40), a title generally reserved for God the Father.

The universalism of the parable ("all the nations") has made it suspect as *ipsissima verba* of Jesus, and there are heavy signs of Matthean redaction. Recent attempts to salvage authenticity include (1) the suggestion that the story belongs between Matthew 10:42 and 11:1 and originally referred to the "house of Israel" which was not receiving Jesus' messengers (10:40–42); and (2) the defense that Jesus took the sort of scene depicted in the Assumption of Moses (where the Gentiles stand before God to be *punished*) and revised it to suggest that it is rather his Jewish critics who will be condemned (so, respectively, Mattill and Bligh). But as the parable stands, it is located in chapter 25 and speaks of all the Gentiles (or nations). In contrast to these views, Bundy points to "its strong social sense" as suggesting an "origin in the Christian proletariat." One may wish, with a host of critics, to trace a core back to Jesus and allow for development in the early church and by Matthew.

Among the stumbling blocks in the pericope for many a modern is what Darwin called the "damnable doctrine" of "eternal punishment" (changed by the Jehovah's Witnesses translation to "annihilation" for doctrinal reasons, but intended by Matthew as a parallel to "eternal life," as a result irrevocable). The implication is, that for all Matthew has said about Jesus Christ, in the last analysis salvation depends on what we have done as good works. A final problem is the suggestion in some

exegeses that Christ here is identifying himself with all the
outcasts of the world, and we thus have "a Christ" to be found in
non-Christian humanity, a humanity which thus becomes
"anonymous Christians."

The context of the passage is all-important. The Sheep and the
Goats is the last of seven parables about the parousia. The first six
are directed to disciples and teach readiness for the judgment
which is sure to come, though not necessarily imminently; cf.
24:32–36 (fig tree), 24:37–42 (the days of Noah), 24:43–44 (the
thief), 25:1–13 (wise and foolish maidens), and 25:14–30 (talents).
This seventh parallel, however, is about Gentiles. Matthew
25:31–46 describes the basis on which *the nations* will be judged
at the final assize. And the criterion, spelled out in a series of first-
person statements, turns out to be the love command (25:35–40,
42–45; cf. 22:34–40). The pagans will be judged on the basis of
the second great command, to love one's neighbor as oneself (Lev.
19:18).

Our reason for saying that the Gentiles are meant in 25:31–46
lies in the fact that the disciples play a different role in this scene:
they are portrayed as the brothers of the king, to whom the
pagans have done deeds of visiting, clothing, feeding, or giving
drink, and thereby, unknowingly, to Jesus himself, the king who
now is judge. Before his throne, in addition to the angels and "the
least of these my brethren," two groups are formed: the sheep,
who helped these brethren, and the goats, who did not. Such an
analysis carries with it the implication that "the Son of man" here
is a corporate figure, and why not, if Daniel 7:13f. is the
background? For in Daniel 7 the Son of man is a collective figure,
representing "the saints of the Most High" (cf. 7:18 with 7:13f.).

Analytically we may say the heart of the scene is the simile at
25:32–33. Envisioned is a separating among Gentiles such as
Matthew elsewhere says will apply to the church at the judgment
(cf. 13:30, 48f.).

The sayings, "I was hungry, thirsty, a stranger, naked, sick, in
prison" (25:35ff.), strike many as having the ring of "the Master
himself" (T. W. Manson). Nevertheless, it is also to be observed
how closely the details follow Paul's catalogue of the sufferings of
a missionary-witness (2 Cor. 11:27, "in hunger and thirst, often

without food"; 1 Cor. 4:11, "hunger and thirst, . . . ill-clad and buffeted and homeless," 4:9–10, "weak," "sentenced to death"; 2 Cor. 11:23, imprisonments, beatings, near death; for "stranger," cf. 3 John 5 and the description in 2 Cor. 11:26). In the background, therefore, lurk the patterns of the early Christian mission and its hardships. All this Matthew has built into a scene framed by Old Testament language and Matthean concepts (e.g., v. 31 reflects Zech. 14:5 and Matt. 13:41, 16:27 (cf. *Proclamation* or other commentaries).

What Matthew has put together in this tableau is a depiction of what will happen at the judgment to the Gentiles who have not yet heard the good news about the kingdom of heaven or taken to themselves its blessedness or the yoke of its imperatives. They will be judged by the way they have treated "the least of these, the brethren" of the king.

The most likely view is that those whom the Gentiles helped (or failed to aid) were the Christians. "Brethren" in Matthew is a synonym for disciple (12:49; 23:8). The superlative, "the least," is either the equivalent of "the little ones" (cf. 5:19; 10:42; 18:6, 10, 14) or, if the superlative degree is to be pressed, the most important members of the community (cf. 23:11; 20:26f.), but in any case disciples. Very likely they are the missionary members of the group whom Jesus sends forth (10:5ff.; 28:19–20). We should not be surprised that Jesus identifies so closely with them (25:40, 45), for the promise to disciples is that he will be with them (18:20; 28:20).

Thus the judgment of the Gentiles rests upon the way they treated Jesus' messengers and thereby Jesus himself. The rabbinic precept holds that "an agent is as the one who sent him" (cf. 10:40–42; 18:5). Small wonder that one recent article on this pericope was called, "What the World Owes the Church." Matthew, of course, has kept his concept of mission and world from all triumphalism by the sort of Christology and nonhierarchical, unpresumptuous model of discipleship on which he insists.

It needs to be added, however, that some exegetes equate "the least of these my brethren" not with Christians but with all the least and lost and disenfranchised of the world. This then allows all pagans to be somehow "anonymous Christians," where the Christ is to be sought in the masses of humankind, presumably also by Christians. Such an exegesis reverses the reading of Matthew given above and finds the Christ not in his community but in the world, and lets Christians be judged on the basis of their works to these peoples.

This is a bold interpretation but it cannot be exegetically sustained. See Father Vawter's aside in *Proclamation* on the arrogance of assuming "anonymous Christians," and Fuller's remark that our interpretation "will disappoint, perhaps even anger many, but we are responsible for a genuine exegesis of the text, not to make it say what we want to hear" (pp. 280–81).

If this is so, how does the allegory about the sheep and the goats help spur Christians on in the quest for social justice or a change in lifestyle in the face of the population dilemma? (1) Note how this passage does "protect us against . . . righteousness through intellectualized theology," just as 20:1–6 keeps us from righteousness via works (E. Schweizer). Matthew 25:31–46 keeps us from sneering at "'secular' charity that does not include a confession of faith." And we shall never solve the population challenge on a confessional or even just a Christian basis.

(2) This parable, along with the six preceding it, reminds us of the seriousness of God's judgment over the church as well as the world. Matthew is clear that disciples of Jesus will be judged too, for their stewardship (25:14–30), alertness (25:1–13), and, yes, exemplary style of humble, self-effacing life. Have you been salt and light for the world? Matthew has created a kind of "ethical prophecy" which will continue to trouble a church which does not obey its Lord.

(3) We must note the high esteem in which the pagans are held, not just as objects of conversion but, even if they have not heard (due, maybe, to our delinquencies) the kerygma or responded, they are sheep of the king's flock and blessed to inherit a kingdom long ago prepared. This high estimate of how "the heathen" can and do respond on issues of justice and ministering care ought to encourage us to work with peoples of other faiths or of no religion.

A Christian community can work with the nations of God's

world, knowing that it too is under judgment (in the same "lifeboat"). A Christian community can be optimistic about those who do not share the gospel as it works with them toward tackling problems like population increase, even if we have no biblical blueprint for a precise answer.

FURTHER READINGS:

Kaiser, Otto. *Isaiah 13–39. The Old Testament Library.* Trans. R.A. Wilson. Philadelphia: Westminster Press, 1974.

Westermann, Claus. *Isaiah 40–66. The Old Testament Library.* Trans. D.M.G. Stalker. Philadelphia: Westminster Press, 1969.

On Matthew 25, in addition to the commentaries of E. Schweizer, *The Good News According to Matthew.* Atlanta: John Knox Press, 1975, and H.B. Green, New Clarendon Bible, 1975, see T.W. Manson in Major-Manson-Wright, *The Mission and Message of Jesus.* New York: Dutton, 1938, pp. 540–44; W.E. Bundy, *Jesus and the First Three Gospels.* Cambridge, Mass.: Harvard University Press, 1955, pp. 475f.; and J. Jeremias, *The Parables of Jesus.* New York: Scribners, 1963, pp. 206–10. Also:

Robinson, John A.T. "The 'Parable' of the Sheep and the Goats," *NTS* 2 (1956), pp. 225–37, reprinted in *Twelve New Testament Studies* (SBT 34; 1962), pp. 76–93.

Bligh, Philip H. "Eternal Fire, Eternal Punishment, Eternal Life (Mt. 25:41, 46)," *Expository Times* 83 (1971–72), pp. 9–11.

Mattill, A.J., Jr. "What the World Owes the Church," *Homiletical and Pastoral Review* 71 (1971), pp. 8–17.

———. "Matthew 25:31–46 Relocated," *Restoration Quarterly* 17 (1974), pp. 107–14.

Mánek, Jindřich. "Mit wem identifiziert sich Jesus? Eine exegetische Rekonstruktion ad Matt. 25:31–46." *Christ and Spirit in the New Testament.* C.F.D. Moule Festschrift; Cambridge University Press, 1973, pp. 15–25 (Eng. summary).

Alternative Views of Priorities in Population Policy

Arthur J. Dyck*

DEBATES over the nature of population problems and the kinds of population policies needed to respond to these problems generate a great deal of heat. Deep differences of opinion are not in themselves surprising or disturbing when complex social problems and policies designed to alleviate them are under discussion. However, there is an especially urgent need to analyze population policy debates because of the serious nature of the disagreements that exist and the serious consequences either of choosing the wrong policies or of choosing none.

In this essay, I will describe as clearly as possible the significant sources of agreement and disagreement about population policy. This will involve a description of three major groups whose population policy recommendations vie for acceptance; crisis environmentalists, family planners, and developmental distributivists. These three groups represent distinct policy orientations and priorities.

The recommendations associated with the orientations are not necessarily mutually exclusive, however. For example, family planners may also favor policies being recommended by developmental distributivists. At the same time, there are family

*The author is Mary B. Saltonstall Professor of Population Ethics, School of Public Health; member of the faculty, Divinity School; and co-director, Kennedy Interfaculty Program in Medical Ethics, Harvard University, Cambridge, Massachusetts. This article is reprinted from *BioScience* 27: pp. 272–276, April 1977.

planners who are sympathetic to some of the analyses of crisis environmentalists.

I am not concerned here with these overlapping allegiances, but rather with how these three distinct orientations within debates concerning population policy shape our understanding of population problems and what responses to them are morally appropriate. After analyzing these views, I will briefly assess what appear to be the most cogent moral priorities for guiding population policy.

When I speak here of "policy recommendations," I am referring to recommendations that specify a responsible agency, a goal, and appropriate means for its realization (Potter, *War and Moral Discourse*, p. 23). In this essay, the focus is on three different orientations toward what are considered to be population-influencing policies.

CRISIS ENVIRONMENTALISTS

One group of thinkers takes the view that rapid population growth has already produced a serious crisis for the human species and the planet Earth. Some, such as Paul Ehrlich (*The Population Bomb;* Ehrlich and Ehrlich, *Population, Resources, and Environment*), emphasize resource depletion, pollution, and environmental degradation. Others, like William and Paul Paddock (*Famine 1975*), concentrate more specifically on depletion of food resources and, in 1967, predicted widespread famine in 1975. Garrett Hardin ("The Tragedy of the Commons") has stressed all of these themes as consequences of rapid population growth. These thinkers and those who share their viewpoints assume that population growth is likely to continue and even escalate in the absence of explicit governmental constraint or mutually agreed-upon coercion. They all agree that resources needed for the survival of the human species are finite and will be depleted unless population is held at a level that establishes a favorable balance between numbers of people and available resources.

The key empirical assumption that characterizes crisis environmentalists is that as population increases, pollution, resource depletion, and environmental damage increase. Indeed, this group is virtually convinced that the number of people on the earth already exceeds the optimal level. The environmental threats to human survival are exacerbated, therefore, by every increase in that number, and the problems associated with these increases may at any time become irreversibly lethal because of the finite nature of the earth. Ehrlich expressed this in a very simple and clear formula: the environment is sick, the disease is overpopulation, the remedy is population control, using coercion as necessary.

It is not immediately evident that population density is the only or the most important factor in bringing about environmental degradation. Why then do crisis environmentalists focus on overpopulation as the critical factor in environmental problems? Why also does societal or governmental coercion appear to be necessary? Ehrlich's writings implicitly assume that economic interests and pollution on the part of large corporations are more difficult to change or control than individual fertility behavior.

Even so, the interest that people take in having children is strong and may require governmental sanctions if birth rates are to be reduced. Kingsley Davis ("Population Policy") and Garrett Hardin have contended that there is no logical reason to expect individual couples to decide on an average family size that will be congruent with societal expectations or needs. Davis based his argument largely on the discrepancy between family size desired and achieved on the one hand and the family size norm necessary for approaching and achieving zero population growth on the other. However, there is an assumption, explicitly articulated by Hardin, that the kind of self-interest that individuals invest in their children is such that society's interest in children is not and cannot be congruent with those of individuals.

The appeal to survival is at the heart of the moral justifications that crisis environmentalists offer for coercive population policies. Some of the policies mentioned in this literature include economic incentives, both positive and negative[1] (Pohlman, "Incentives"), compulsory abortion in certain cases (Davis; Ehrlich and Ehrlich), triage in matters of food policy (Greene,

1. For a noncrisis-oriented, careful sorting out of ethical issues raised by incentive policies, see Robert M. Veatch, "Governmental Incentives."

"Triage"; Hardin; Paddock and Paddock), and antifertility chemicals in water supplies (Ketchel, "Fertility Control Agents").

FAMILY PLANNERS

Although crisis environmentalists have received considerable publicity, the family planners have had the ear of governments in the United States and in numerous countries throughout the world.[2] The family-planning movement in the United States, founded by Margaret Sanger and others in the early twentieth century, has since been exported all over the world by planned parenthood organizations (Piotrow, *World Population Crisis*).

The thinking of family planners is well represented within the Report of the U.S. Commission on Population Growth and the American Future (1972) and within the official global policies of the Population Division of the U.S. Agency for International Development (AID). (See, for example, Claxton and Costa, *Statement* and U.S. House of Representatives, "U.S. Aid," 1973.) What, then, are the major tenets of family planners and what are their specific objections to the views of crisis environmentalists?

Family planners, like crisis environmentalists, sometimes speak of overpopulation, but more often focus upon unwanted fertility or rapid population growth. They have gathered data in many regions of the world, which at first glance support the view that in every country and in most families parents have children that they do not want. These data also allegedly indicate widespread favorable attitudes toward the use of birth control methods.[3] Family planners have concluded that if governments make these methods and the knowledge of their use readily and freely available to everyone, people would have fewer children.

Sometimes family planners, particularly within the context of the Population Commission Report and the publications of AID,

---

2. Annually since 1969, the Population Council has published reviews of family-planning activities in governments around the world. See, for example, Dorothy Nortman and Ellen Hofstatter, "Population and Family Planning Programs."

3. KAP (Knowledge, Attitudes and Practices) studies in particular seek to document these contentions. For a criticism of these studies and the conclusions drawn from them, see Anthony Marino, "K.A.P. Surveys."

amass arguments specifically designed to persuade people to have small families and to consider them ideal. Hence, such literature discusses the undesirability of large families: the larger the family, the more difficult it is to deal with poverty, to provide education for one's children, to accumulate savings for investments, and to maintain the health of mothers and of the children who might be born. All of these empirical claims argue that it is in the interest of each family to practice family planning and to stay small.

The Population Commission set zero population growth as a desirable goal for the United States. Yet despite this, family planners, unlike crisis environmentalists, do not recommend coercive government policies. On the contrary, they favor complete voluntarism in the form of government investment in free-standing birth control clinics to offer all the available methods of birth control to those who would not otherwise be able to afford them. The Population Commission proposed an expenditure of $1.8 billion for the fiscal years 1974–78 inclusive for that purpose, more than 10 times as much as the $150 million it recommended for continuing the governmental provision of maternal and child health clinics (U.S. Commission on Population Growth 1972, p. 188). In the light of their research on unwanted fertility, family planners expect individuals to use these governmental services for reducing family size and population growth in the United States and throughout the world.

There are two additional, significant reasons why family planners do not advocate coercion and why they trust that governmental provision of birth control services will approach zero population growth. First, family planners assume there is no serious conflict between individuals and society; couples are expected to have fewer children and thus move their societies toward zero population growth. The belief that individual interests and societal interests will ultimately harmonize is completely at odds with the assumption of crisis environmentalists that such interests ultimately conflict. This difference provides one important rationale for the tendency of family planners to reject a crisis orientation.

The second reason family planners disavow coercion is that they put a strong value on freedom. Freedom for them largely means absence of governmental constraints. In keeping with this view, the Population Commission and family planners generally advocate the removal of any existing impediments, including monetary costs, which would hinder anyone from access to abortion, sterilization, and contraceptive services (U.S. Commission on Population Growth 1972, chap. 11).

DEVELOPMENTAL DISTRIBUTIVISTS

This group is characterized by its belief that certain kinds of improvements in socioeconomic conditions lead to lower birth rates as observed in "the demographic transition" experienced in Western countries. Whereas crisis environmentalists and family planners stress the unfavorable socioeconomic consequences of large families and rapid population growth, developmental distributivists have seen unfavorable socioeconomic conditions as major *causes* of large families and rapid population growth. Developmental distributivists take the view that illiteracy (especially of women), high infant mortality rates, extremely unjust distributions of income, lack of governmental social security systems, underemployment, and poor production in agriculture are some of the most important socioeconomic conditions that contribute to high fertility rates and rapid population growth. These are precisely the causal links stressed in the World Plan of Action adopted at Bucharest (Population Council Report, 1974).

Developmental distributivists are not arguing that general improvements in socioeconomic conditions as measured by levels of per capita income or per capita GNP will by themselves bring about lower fertility rates. The key to lowering fertility lies in the extensiveness of the distribution of benefits (Kocher, *Rural Development;* Rich, *Smaller Families*). As William Rich pointed out, countries have lowered fertility where these benefits involve a relatively equitable distribution of health and education services and of land, credit, and other income opportunities; the cumulative effect is that the poorest half of the population is vastly better off than it is in countries with equal or higher levels of per capita GNP but poor distribution patterns.

Demographers have long theorized that the change to low birth rates in Western countries (the demographic transition) was associated with low infant mortality rates, high literacy rates, and processes of modernization that included such developments as higher income and better income distribution, improved agriculture, and the provision of social security. Furthermore, there is evidence to suggest that the demographic transition that occurred in the more affluent countries of the West will also occur as a result of socioeconomic development in currently less affluent nations. Indeed, Dudley Kirk's analysis ("A New Demographic Transition?") concludes that a growing number of countries are entering a demographic transition at a somewhat faster rate than was true of Western countries. Family planners have cited a number of these countries as experiencing significant declines in birth rates and attribute these declines to the introduction of family-planning programs (see, e.g., Ravenholt et al., "Family Planning Programs"). Developmental distributivists, however, examining the same data, point out that every one of these countries is experiencing important gains in distributing socioeconomic benefits and that it is precisely under these conditions that people use family-planning programs to reduce birth rates.

Recently Michael Teitelbaum ("Population and Development") spoke of a new consensus that population policies should combine family-planning programs and socioeconomic development. But from the point of view of developmental distributivists, not just any kind of socioeconomic development, whether or not it is combined with family-planning programs, will yield lower birth rates. Brazil and Mexico with much higher per capita income continue to have high birth and growth rates, whereas countries like Sri Lanka and Taiwan had falling birth and growth rates with considerably lower levels of per capita income (Kocher; Murdoch and Oaten, "Population and Food"; Rich). The difference lies in the type of socioeconomic development. Sri Lanka and Taiwan have raised the employment and income of the very poorest sectors of their societies and have greatly increased the distribution of income and social services as well.

Furthermore, where we do have controlled studies, family-planning programs by themselves, even with high acceptance rates for birth control methods offered, do not lower birth rates. This is what John Wyon found in a carefully controlled field study conducted in the Punjab area of India from 1953–60 (Wyon and Gordon, *The Khanna Study*; see also Cobb et al., "An I.U.D.", a five-year study in Pakistan). In the late '60s, Wyon returned to the villages he had studied earlier and discovered that birth rates were lower. Apparently, with the coming of the Green Revolution to the Punjab, people were experiencing higher income, more education (especially for girls), and less infant deaths (Wyon and Gordon, *Khanna*; see also Repetto, "The Interaction of Fertility").

Even in understanding the reasons for malnutrition, how wealth is distributed may be more important than population growth. India is the favorite example of overpopulation according to crisis environmentalists. However, there is evidence that in the nineteenth century famines were due to genuine food shortages, but those in the twentieth century are due to distribution problems and the high price of food in periods of relative scarcity (Bhatia, *Famines in India*). As in many economically developing countries, Indian food production is increasing faster than population (Gavan and Dixon, "The Food Situation in India"; see also Revelle, "Food and Population"). But poor people starve or are malnourished in India, as in other countries, because they lack the money or the knowledge to feed themselves properly. For example, withholding solid foods from infants in their first two years of life is a major cause of infant mortality (Wyon and Gordon). No reduction in birth rates will by itself affect this cause of malnutrition.

Revelle has calculated that it is technically possible to feed 38 to 48 billion people in this world, 10 to 13 times the present population. The point is that people starve because of the policies their governments pursue and because of their poverty and lack of knowledge, not because of a lack of food or potential for producing it.

Developmental distributivists do agree with the family planners that in procreative matters the interests of individuals and couples will more or less correspond to the interests of their societies. However, unlike the family planners, developmental distributivists do not expect this to happen by itself or through policies that make all existing birth control methods available to everyone. For them, the interests of individuals and of their societies can only be expected to harmonize when some reasonable degree of social justice has been realized. Developmental distributivists do not accept a notion of freedom that focuses exclusively on absence of constraint. If people are to be free, they must also have the ability and means to make choices and participate in the opportunities available within a given society. Having a small family, for example, makes sense if one can be relatively certain that one's children will have opportunities for health care, education, and future employment.

Social justice as a requisite of population policy is the moral outlook characteristic of developmental distributivists. Marx, Engels, and subsequent Marxists rejected Malthus and subsequent Malthusians precisely in the name of social justice. At Bucharest, Marxists, Roman Catholics, and the great majority of representatives from various countries found themselves allied against the family-planning ideology reflected in the views of the United States and its supporters.[4] What united these groups was the view that social justice in the form of better health care, better income distribution, better status for women, provision for the aged, and the like constitute population policies that lower birth rates.

MORAL CONSIDERATIONS:
VITAL TO POPULATION POLICY

From the foregoing analysis, it should be evident that there is no clear agreement as to what or how serious population related problems are. It is not difficult to agree that the earth cannot

---

4. For official Roman Catholic affinity for stressing the centrality of social justice as a population policy, see Pope Paul VI's Encyclical *Populorum Progressio* (1967).

sustain an indefinite number of people and that, therefore, there is a hypothetical condition called "overpopulation." But there is not agreement on how societies achieve and maintain zero population growth where this seems to be a reasonable goal for a given society.

To answer this kind of question, it is necessary to initiate and study population-influencing policies designed to solve some problems considered to be population related. One of the frustrations of the current analyses of family-planning programs is that these programs do not, by and large, include sufficient data collection and the use of controls that would settle the debates over their alleged successes and failures. The two controlled studies available on the failure of family-planning programs (Cobb et al., "I.U.D."; Wyon and Gordon, *Khanna*) are suggestive but not sufficient in scope to warrant sweeping generalizations about the inefficacy of such programs. Nor do we have any evidence that serious social ills are population related, that the kinds of incentive programs and various forms of compulsion being suggested by some crisis environmentalists would actually work if they were adopted. No programs of this sort were recommended or even mentioned in the World Plan of Action at Bucharest.

How does one choose the scientific studies and social experiments that will deal with some of the serious problems thought to be population related? It seems to me that the decision rests largely on moral grounds.

At this very point, crisis environmentalists would tend to object. They would argue that population related problems have put us into an immediate crisis and threaten the most basic moral value, namely, the value of life itself and the survival of the whole human species. Now I agree that the value of life is fundamental, and I assume that readers and the other population orientations share the desire to strive for the survival of the human species. But is it population growth as such that poses an immediate threat to human survival?

Environmental Degradation

Consider first the problem of environmental degradation. The relationships between population variables and environmental degradation are extremely complex, to say the least. As Roger Revelle ("Paul Ehrlich," p. 68) has noted:

> More than half of the environmental deterioration in the United States since 1940 . . . had resulted from our growing affluence and changes in consumption patterns—from our increasingly filthy habits. For example, one of the major sources of pollution is the growth of electric power generation from the burning of sulphur containing coal and oil, which rose about fivefold between 1940 and 1965, while the population was growing by 47 percent. With the per capita power consumption of 1970, . . . our population would have to be reduced to 20 million souls to arrive at the same total power consumption as in 1940.

The point of this analysis is that pollution and affluence grow much faster than the population, and pollution grows as affluence grows. If, as many population experts assert, decreasing population growth will increase affluence, then decreasing population growth will increase environmental deterioration, unless, of course, our present modes of production, consumption, and waste disposal are changed. Developmental distributivists and others have argued, therefore, that our current habits and not population growth by itself are at the heart of those environmental problems that can be considered serious.

Clearly, constraints on our wastefulness and pollution will need to become part of modern industrial life. Scientists contribute to human welfare and survival by documenting these necessities and constraints. However, crisis environmentalists have done us a disservice by giving us simplified, even factually false, accounts of the way in which population and environmental variables interact. Indeed, some scientists like Ehrlich and Ehrlich (*Population, Resources, and Environment*) have made astounding factual errors in their calculations of strains on our environment. A number of these have been documented by Revelle, such as misstatements of the need for water in the United States, errors in estimating annual fish production, large overstatements of the existence of DDT in the environment, etc.

If scientists are to have credibility with the public, their peers, and political decision makers, they will have to maintain the commitment of science to truth-telling and precision. J. Bronowski (*Science and Human Values*, p. 66) sees this as an essential element in scientific practice and morality:

> . . . If I let myself believe anything on insufficient evidence, there may be no great harm done by the mere belief; it may be true after all, or I may never have occasion to exhibit it in outward acts. But I cannot help doing this great wrong towards Man, that I make myself credulous. The danger to society is not merely that it should believe wrong things, though that is great enough; but that it should become credulous.

Garrett Hardin is another crisis environmentalist who has strained the usual limits of credibility, using his lifeboat metaphor. As Murdoch and Oaten ("Population and Food") correctly pointed out, we are not at all in a lifeboat situation, and for the U.S.A. to take a lifeboat stance at this time would not only be politically detrimental, but also it would worsen the current situation of some nations and contribute to maintaining high birth rates through exacerbating conditions of poverty.

Furthermore, environmental scientists should clarify whether they really consider essential environmental resources finite and nonrenewable. Limiting population growth in any given generation is not nearly so important if the basic necessities of life are finite and nonrenewable. If we do have enough renewable resources to keep the human species viable for a great number of subsequent generations, then it is, of course, important to consider our responsibilities over many generations. Under these circumstances, the depletion of certain finite and nonrenewable resources means the loss of a particular pattern of consumption or lifestyle, and not death for the species.

Freedom and Justice

Family planners have stressed the value of freedom in the form of absence of constraint. They have collected data that lend credence to the possibility of maintaining voluntarism in population policy. I have no quarrel with this aim and the value that propels it. However, family-planning programs and the moral basis on which they are predicated are inadequate.

Consider certain insufficiencies in the moral basis of current family-planning policies of the United States. On their face, these policies would seem to be beneficial; to some degree, where they meet definite needs, they are. But family planners have not given ample attention to the special conditions associated with poverty, which make the free availability of birth control methods something less than a clear benefit. As developmental distributivists have indicated, there are many circumstances under which the poor need children for labor and for security in old age. Also, it is the poor who will lose some of their children through disease and malnutrition. These conditions of poverty are not eliminated by having small families. Therefore, the provision of birth control techniques and knowledge for the poor without changing their circumstances in any other respect may fail to improve or may even worsen their situation. Is such a policy, then, a violation of justice?

From a certain utilitarian perspective, one could argue that justice will have been obtained if family-planning policies serve to bring about the greatest good for the greatest number, even though some of those who are least well off in the society may not directly benefit. But even if family-planning policies were efficacious in lowering birth rates, the fact that for some these policies were disadvantageous could be construed as a violation of the basic principles of justice. As the philosopher John Rawls (A Theory of Justice) has argued, the fairness of a policy depends on whether at least in part the implementation of that policy is advantageous to everyone, not simply the greatest number of persons affected by it.

SUGGESTED POLICIES

The following types of policies were suggested at Bucharest. From the standpoint of justice and also from the standpoint of what appear to be population related variables, they deserve a chance in countries concerned about population growth as well as in countries where these policies have not as yet been implemented to any significant degree:

—good health services available to all, including contraceptive services in the context of providing care for the whole family;

—literacy and nutritional education, especially for women,

where there are inequities in this respect (this policy along with the policy above would have the effect of reducing infant and maternal mortality);

—labor-intensive development, particularly in the agricultural sphere;

—equality for women;

—social security systems, which provide for the aged in ways that do not make them dependent upon the survival and prosperity of their children;

—improvements in the distribution of income and income-earning opportunities.

Each one of these policies is in itself advantageous to those who are now disadvantaged. Each one is also potentially a population-influencing policy in the direction of lowering birth rates. Each has its own moral justification, although the specific form this would take is subject to debate and would need to be elaborated. The extent to which any or all of these can be implemented will, of course, depend upon the resources available to any society that seeks to do so.

What I have tried to argue in only a preliminary and suggestive way is that these policies have relevance to what are considered to be population related issues. At the same time they are ingredients in the realization of social justice by providing advantages to the relatively disadvantaged. There is no decisive evidence that they will or will not work as population policies. There is evidence, however, that the notion of justice implicit in them is one which the large bulk of the world's population clearly understands and endorses.

REFERENCES CITED

Bhatia, B.M. *Famines in India: 1860–1965.* New York: Asia Publishing House, 1967.

Bronowski, J. *Science and Human Values,* rev. ed. New York: Harper and Row, 1965.

Claxton, P.P., Jr., and M.A. Costa. "Statement by the Delegation of the United States of America." Second Asian Population Conference, Tokyo, 1–13 November, 1972.

Cobb, J.C., H.M. Roulet, and P. Harper. "An I.U.D. Field Trial in Lulliani, West Pakistan." Paper presented at the American Public Health Association, 21 October, 1965.

Davis, K. "Population Policy: Will Current Programs Succeed?" *Science* 158 (1969), pp. 730–739.

Ehrlich, P. *The Population Bomb.* New York: Ballentine Books, 1968.

Ehrlich, P., and A. Ehrlich. *Population, Resources, and Environment: Issues in Human Ecology.* San Francisco: W. H. Freeman, 1970.

Gavin, J., and J. Dixon. "The Food Situation in India: a Perspective." Unpublished essay, Harvard Center for Population Studies, October 1974.

Greene, W. "Triage: Who Shall be Fed? Who Shall Starve?" *New York Times Magazine,* January 9, 1975.

Hardin, G. "The Tragedy of the Commons," *Science* 162 (1968), pp. 1243–1248.

_____. "Living on a Lifeboat," *BioScience* 24 (1974), pp. 561–568.

Ketchel, M.M. "Fertility Control Agents as a Possible Solution to the World Population Problem," *Perspect. Biol. Med.* 11 (1968), pp. 687–703.

Kirk, D. "A New Demographic Transition?" in *Rapid Population Growth: Consequences and Policy Implications.* Baltimore: Johns Hopkins Press, 1971, pp. 123–147.

Kocher, J. *Rural Development, Income Distribution and Fertility Decline.* An occasional paper of the Population Council. Bridgeport, Conn.: Key Book Service, 1973.

Marino, A. "K.A.P. Surveys and the Politics of Family Planning," *Concerned Demography* 3(1) (1971), pp. 36–75.

Murdoch, W.W., and A. Oaten. "Population and Food: Metaphors and the Reality," *BioScience* 25 (1975), pp. 561–567.

Nortman, D., and E. Hofstatter. "Population and Family Planning Programs: a Factbook." *Reports on Population/Family Planning.* New York: The Population Council, December 1974.

Paddock, W., and P. Paddock. *Famine 1975.* Boston: Little Brown & Company, 1967.

Piotrow, P.T. *World Population Crisis: The United States Response.* New York: Praeger Publishers, 1973.

Pohlman, E. "Incentives: not Ideal, but Necessary," in J. Philip Wogaman, ed. *The Population Crisis and Moral Responsibility.* Washington, D.C.: Public Affairs Press, 1973, pp. 225–232.

Pope Paul VI. *Populorum Progressio,* Encyclical. Boston: Daughters of St. Paul, 1967.

Population Council. Appendix to A Report on Bucharest. *Stud. Fam. Plan.* 5 (1974), pp. 381–395.

Potter, R.B. *War and Moral Discourse.* Richmond, Va.: John Knox Press, 1969.

Ravenholt, R.T., J.W. Brackett, and J. Chao. "Family Planning Programs and Fertility Patterns." *Family Planning Programs.* Population Report, Series J., No. 1, August 1973. Department of

Medical and Public Affairs, George Washington University Medical Center, Washington, D.C.

Rawls, J. *A Theory of Justice.* Cambridge, Mass.: Harvard University Press, 1971.

Repetto, R. "The Interaction of Fertility and the Size Distribution of Income." Research Paper No. 8, October 1974. Harvard Center for Population Studies, Cambridge, Mass.

Revelle, R. "Paul Ehrlich: New High Priest of Ecocatastrophe," *Fam. Planning Perspec.* 3 (1971) p. 68.

――――. "Food and population." *Sci. Amer.* 231 (1974) pp. 160–170.

Rich, W. *Smaller Families Through Social Economic Progress.* Monograph No. 7 of the Overseas Development Council, Washington, D.C., January 1973.

Teitelbaum, M.S. "Population and Development: Is a Consensus Possible?" *Foreign Affairs,* July 1974, pp. 742–760.

U.S. Commission on Population Growth and the American Future. *Population and the American Future.* New York: Signet Books, New American Library, Inc., 1972.

U.S. House of Representatives. "U.S. aid to population/family planning in Asia." Report of a staff survey team to the Committee on Foreign Affairs, U.S. House of Representatives, 93rd Cong., 1st Sess., 25 February, 1973, U.S. Government Printing Office, Washington, D.C.

Veatch, R.M. "Governmental Incentives: Ethical Issues at Stake," in J. Philip Wogaman, ed. *The Population Crisis and Moral Responsibility.* Washington, D.C.: Public Affairs Press, 1973.

Wyon, J.B., and J.E. Gordon. *The Khanna Study.* Cambridge, Mass.: Harvard University Press, 1971.

Numbering the Sand on the Seashore

Elizabeth A. Bettenhausen *

IN a recent address a bishop of West Germany reported that material affluence and self-interest had combined to create a serious problem in Germany. The birth rate had dropped so low that the bishops of the church found it necessary to remind parishioners of their "Christian responsibility" to reproduce.

In the April 1978 issue of an airline magazine an article

*The author is Secretary for Social Concerns, Department for Church and Society, Division for Mission in North America of the Lutheran Church in America.

summarized projections by sociologists, economists, and demographers that predict a baby boom by 1985 in the United States. Contingent on another prediction of "good times and prosperity" by the 1980s, the baby boom is put at five million births in 1990. The baby food industry is already planning new products to capitalize on the growing market. There is no mention in the article of the ethical dimensions of continued population growth in this highly developed, affluent nation.

In January of 1978 *The New York Times* reported that several African countries were experiencing dangerously low birth rates. The apparent cause was venereal disease, especially among the male population. The greatly increased incidence of temporary or permanent sterility was traced to a migration to urban areas and an increase in population, evidence of the impact of "Western" values on traditional morality.

In a report on the remarkable decline in fertility and mortality rates in the state of Kerala in southern India, John W. Ratcliffe, a population researcher, wrote, "In terms of social and economic development strategies, Kerala's successes have been achieved not by the allocation of *more* resources, but rather through a more equitable distribution of *existing* resources, goods, and services. And the distributive political economy which distinguishes Kerala so clearly from other states has also been largely responsible for mortality and fertility declines."[1]

What emerges from the above accounts is a warning. It is dangerous to speak too quickly of "the world's population," as if it constituted one society which would be the subject of ethical deliberation and action on population growth and decline. The population "crisis" in West Germany and parts of Africa is one of low birth rates. The crisis in other areas is declining mortality rates coupled with relatively high fertility rates. In other places the crisis may be a combination of increasing fertility rates over against already excessive consumption rates.

A full understanding of the population issue is still in the future. It is not sufficient to understand the process of contraception. Other factors also play a part in the growth and

1. John W. Ratcliffe, "Poverty, Politics, and Fertility: The Anomaly of Kerala," in *The Hastings Center Report*, 7, Number 1, (1977).

decline of populations, factors which loom like shadowed mountains behind the neat charts of fertility and mortality rates, migration patterns, and graphs of the exponential population growth.

Such graphs and figures do not interpret themselves. The controversy about the definition and extent of the "population question" is not over details of the data. Rather, the disagreement stems from different sets of assumptions from which the data are interpreted. These assumptions have to do with political and economic structures, the ownership and distribution of land, and even the very nature of human beings as individual persons and members of social structures.

One's perspective is crucial in dealing with the population issue. What follows is a description of some factors that form a perspective based on Christian social responsibility. This will be followed by a description of various major groups in the current population debate and their perspectives. Finally, there will be a discussion of the limitations and assets of Christian social teaching in addressing population issues.

Because the topic before us is so serious, it is salutary to keep in mind the perspective of comedian Woody Allen. In a summary description of a typical college course bulletin, he wrote the following for a "Fundamental Astronomy" course: "A detailed study of the universe and its care and cleaning. The sun, which is made of gas, can explode at any moment, sending our entire planetary system hurtling to destruction; students are advised what the average citizen can do in such a case."[2]

A PERSPECTIVE OF CHRISTIAN
SOCIAL RESPONSIBILITY

In confessing the first article of the Apostles' Creed, Christians affirm that God is the creator of life. In the past, difficulties with this confession usually arose in the area of theodicy, the proclamation of the goodness of God in view of the existence of evil. The problems of high mortality rates because of disease and natural disasters and the problems of individual human beings

2. Woody Allen, *Getting Even* (New York: Warner, 1972), p. 49.

born deformed raised questions about the goodness of the Creator. It is only in recent decades that Christians have needed to think about the intermediate steps between the assertion that God creates life and the problems of overpopulation.

To state that God creates human life is a theological assertion. But it is erroneous to conclude that there is a direct, causal connection between God's will and each and every human conception. To state that God loves every human being is also a theological assertion. It is erroneous to conclude that God wills unlimited numbers of people to exist. Very slowly we are beginning to understand that the reproduction of the species is, in its specifics, the responsibility of human beings. The final state of the species on this planet is hidden in God's wisdom. Until then Christian social responsibility must deal with controlling the numbers so that justice and peace may be served.

It is also part of Christian confession that God wills human life on this planet to be physically and spiritually just. Here too human beings are held responsible. We do not know the "optimum" number of human beings on the planet. We do not know for two reasons: first, we are not agreed on the specific components of a physically and spiritually just life for all persons; second, our finite understanding is unable to know the boundaries of the resources necessary to maintain those components. It is not self-evident that either preventing more births or avoiding more births will lead us to knowledge in those cases.

We can, however, make some confident assertions about the persons now alive. The basic necessities of life must be met for all people. Starkly stated, a concern for justice challenges both our present systems for the distribution of resources and the affluent consumption enjoyed by developed nations. We have not guaranteed food, housing, health care, education, and income security to all people. To the degree that our increasing population will make it even more difficult to meet these needs, the increase should be stopped. We ought not to make the mistake, however, of believing that reduction of birth rates will of itself bring about this basic justice.

The assertion that life should be spiritually just is actually more existential than theological. Although prerequisite, it is not enough that only the physical needs of human beings be met. Justice for the spirit must include opportunity to participate in the political life of the community. It is here that the determination of the means to justice is made. The ability of persons to control human reproduction is in part a function of their ability to decide the uses of power—economic, political, sexual—in their lives. Exclusion from decision-making in these respects is unjust subordination and often the domination of many by the few. It is the opposite of the justice we are enjoined to seek.

Within the perspective of Christian social responsibility the norm of justice is defined by the neighbor's need. From the vantage point of affluent Christians in North America it is particularly useful to describe the positive standard (justice) by pointing to the negative or empty (because lacking) conditions which constitute its absence. If we are unable to describe completely what the perfectly just society would be in detail, we can nonetheless point to the need of the neighbor as something to be met if proximate justice is to be reached. Thus we will be compelled to engage in economic and political action on a scale appropriate to the needs that stare us in the face—wherever basic human rights are being denied.

For such a lifetime task we are not without tools. In the face of a complex of problems labeled "population ethics," Christian social responsibility operates with two biases: we are to favor life (which does not necessarily mean we favor ever increasing numbers of human beings), and we are to pursue justice. But the tool to determine the means to these favored ends is the God-given gift of reason. With regard to population questions, we have the responsibility to define the questions clearly and fairly, to challenge ideologies or demagogic scare tactics, to include all essential aspects of the debate, and to seek reasonable solutions through the participation of all parties affected by the determination of proximate justice.

Part of the responsibility for the careful use of human reason is the use of the corrective possibilities of the community. No matter to what theological theory of the state of reason after the Fall one adheres, in most cases public discussion of individual reasoning improves that reasoning. In social ethics, if not in art, two heads

are better than one. One part of the perspective of Christian
social responsibility should therefore be to bring together into
community discussion persons who no longer seem willing to
speak with one another.

SIDES OF THE PUBLIC
POPULATION DEBATE

There is no unanimity on the nature of the "population
problem." Not even all agree that there is a population "crisis."
Some people, seeking to reach a consensus among the different
views, have described sixteen different stances on the means to
address the complex of population and development.[3] The
consensus position then incorporates the best of all these stances.
Others have described the perspectives in three categories, which,
for our purposes, will serve. The limitation of these categories is
given by Arthur J. Dyck, who states that perspectives can be
distinguished between those which are "population-influencing
policies and population-responsive policies."[4] The three he
describes are population-responsive. This leaves an interim gap,
for even though we may influence population growth in the long
run, we are confronted by virtue of population growth
momentum with the necessity of responding to an inevitable and
significant increase in population growth in the next three
decades of this planet's life. But first, a summary of the ap-
proaches to restricting long-range growth.

As expanded in Dyck's essay in this volume, the three categories
used to describe the debate on population policy are crisis environmentalists, family planners, and developmental distributivists. "The key empirical assumption that characterizes the
crisis environmentalist is that as population increases, pollution,
resource depletion, and environmental damage increase."[5] The

3. Michael S. Teitelbaum, "Population and Development: Is a Consensus
Possible?" in *Foreign Affairs*, July 1974, reprinted in *Ethics in Medicine*, Stanley
Joel Reiser, Arthur J. Dyck, and William J. Curran, eds. (Cambridge, Mass.: The
MIT Press, 1977), p. 340.
4. Arthur J. Dyck, "Assessing the Population Debate," in *The Monist*, January
1977, reprinted in *Ethics in Medicine*, p. 348.
5. *Ibid*, p. 349.

growth in population has, according to this group, reached crisis proportions already; the survival of the planet is at stake.

> . . . crisis environmentalists make the definite anthropological or even quasi-theological assumption that individual interests and societal interests are in a number of critical ways, and certainly in matters of procreation, in conflict with one another. Hence the need for coercion.[6]

The crisis environmentalist position also relies on the argument from the finitude of the earth and its resources to justify the coercion necessary to limit the population. If nothing less than the survival of the human species is at issue, then there is no point in talking about human freedom. Michael S. Teitelbaum has summarized this position as follows:

> The Population Hawk position. Unrestrained population growth is the principal cause of poverty, malnutrition, environmental disruption, and other social problems. Indeed we are faced with impending catastrophe on food and environmental fronts. Such a desperate situation necessitates draconian action to retrain population even if coercion is required. "Mutual coercion, mutually agreed upon."[7]

Dyck's "family planners" position holds that "if governments make birth control methods and the knowledge of their use readily and freely available to everyone, people would have less children."[8] The problem is seen more as unwanted fertility or rapid population growth than overpopulation.

In several key assumptions the family planners differ completely from the crisis environmentalists. They "assume that there is no serious conflict between individuals and society, in that couples are expected to have fewer children and so to move in the direction of zero population growth."[9] Family planners point to data from many parts of the world to support this expectation. In this perspective, governmental coercion is an evil which conflicts directly with the highly valued moral good or individual freedom. In this view the "population problem" is best addressed

---

6. *Ibid.*
7. Teitelbaum, p. 344.
8. Dyck, p. 350.
9. *Ibid.*

by "complete voluntarism in the form of government investment in free-standing birth control clinics to offer all the available methods of birth control to those who would not otherwise be able to afford them."[10]

The third group, developmental distributivists, "is characterized by its belief that certain kinds of improvements in socioeconomic conditions lead to lower birth rates as observed in the 'demographic transition' experienced in Western countries."[11] While crisis environmentalists and family planners look at large families and see them as the cause of bad economic, environmental, and social conditions, the developmental distributivists argue that such conditions are the cause of large population increases.

> Developmental distributivists take the view that illiteracy, especially of women, high infant mortality rates, extremely unjust distributions of income, lack of governmental social security systems, and underemployment and poor production in agriculture are among some of the most important socioeconomic conditions that contribute to high fertility rates and rapid population growth.[12]

This group disagrees with the assumption of the crisis environmentalists that population growth is the primary cause of environmental degradation. They point out that affluence and power consumption in the United States increased far faster than the population in the decades after World War II. The environment is endangered not so much by the sheer numbers of people as by their lifestyles and patterns of conspicuous consumption. On the other hand, this group disagrees with the family planners in that they do not believe that contraception alone will lower the rate of population growth. While agreeing that the interests of individuals and society are not in basic conflict, these interests "can only be expected to harmonize when some reasonable degree of social justice has been realized."[13] Essential to this social justice are "the extensiveness of the

10. *Ibid.*
11. *Ibid*, p. 351.
12. *Ibid.*
13. *Ibid*, p. 352.

distribution of income and of social services"[14] and the full participation of persons in the political decisions necessary to achieve that.

Even from these brief summaries it is clear that basic assumptions about individuals in society, relationships between fertility and economic conditions, and coercion and freedom separate the groups. There is not even agreement on whether we have a population "crisis" or population "problems." What sense are we to make of this debate from the perspective of Christian social responsibility?

LIMITATION AND FREEDOM

Within traditional Christian teaching there are certain aspects which hinder the development of a helpful perspective on these questions. Our Scripture and much of our theology were developed in agrarian societies which had high mortality rates. There is a bias in favor of more births in the ethics which were developed in such a context. We can now only assume that the promise to Abraham about the sands of the seashore and the stars in the heavens was meant figuratively.

In this same context there is another bias which is still very much with us. The role of women in such a perspective is predominantly that of childbearer. Although one hopes that not many now believe with the writer of 1 Timothy that "women will be saved through bearing children" (2:15), there is still in our society intense pressure on women to see their human worth primarily as a function of their maternity. We have just begun to see how this bias affects educational expectations, economic roles, and even nutritional patterns for women, not only in the United States and Canada, but in all countries.

We have also been limited by a reductionist sexual ethic which has focused on reproduction by married couples. We have asserted the family as an order within creation but have neglected the tough ethical problems which are posed in the sexual activity of people who are not part of a married heterosexual pair. For example, we have not begun to deal with the educational challenge posed by sexually active teenagers.

14. *Ibid*, p. 351.

On the other hand, the tradition also frees us to deal responsibly with population questions. Against the "First Timothys" of the world we assert: *sola gratia*. At the heart of the gospel is the assertion that biology is not destiny and we are only beginning to see the implications of this for the role of women in church and society. When the Hebrews turned from the fertility cults of the Ancient Near East and described God as creating through the Word instead of by sexual intercourse, human nature was also understood differently. At that time the males were seen to transcend biological destiny through volition. Millennia later we are beginning to see that through reason and volition women are competent to do the same.

The tradition of Christian social responsibility also enables us to balance matters of individual freedom and government regulation. This is not to say that we have found the means to enable free and responsible choices in reproduction while simultaneously maintaining the common welfare. But we are rightly wary of government coercion that is allegedly justified on grounds of survival, the enslavement of individualistic license, or the inability of persons to control reproduction. While keeping to our understanding of original sin, we do not believe that groups or governments act more justly than individuals.

Finally, we know that neither our reproduction nor our ethics will bring about the eschaton. Unlike Cinderella we will not be carried off in a pumpkin at the stroke of midnight. We do not know the hour, but we know the promise of the End. In the meantime we might devote our attention to evaluating the lifestyle of the ball at which the affluent dance and the powerful parade—and attending to the needs of persons on the planet poorer even than Cinderella.

AN INQUIRY INTO THE HUMAN PROSPECT
by Robert L. Heilbroner. New York: W. W. Norton and Company, Inc., 1975; 180 pp.; $2.25.

Robert L. Heilbroner, Norman Thomas Professor of economics at the New School for Social Research, finds the subject of population one of the three basic problems which make the human prospect seem "painful, difficult, perhaps desperate" (p. 72). The other two are nuclear weaponry and the threat to our environment resulting from resource limitations and pollution problems.

The analysis is cold-blooded and convincing, and he admits with apparent dismay that rationality, the basis of so much of what we call the modern world, sometimes the post-enlightenment world or the scientific world, has little to offer when it comes to concern for the more distant future.

> Economic growth and technical achievement, the greatest triumphs of our epoch of history, have shown themselves to be inadequate sources for collective contentment and hope. Material advance, the most profoundly distinguishing attribute of industrial capitalism and socialism alike, has proved unable to satisfy the human spirit. Not only the quest for profit but the cult of efficiency have shown themselves ultimately corrosive for human well-being. A society dominated by the machine process, dependent on factory and office routine, celebrating itself in the act of individual consumption, is finally insufficient to retain our loyalty (pp. 159f.).

In his most shocking chapter, "What Has Posterity Ever Done For Me?", he articulates the problem with frightening clarity: "Will mankind survive? Who knows? . . . Who cares? It is clear that most of us today do not care—or at least do not care enough" (p. 169). And he continues in the same vein, "Would we care enough for posterity to pay the price of its survival? I doubt it."

Summarizing the attitude of rationality he writes: "Why should I lift a finger to affect events that will have no more meaning for me seventy-five years after my death than those that happened seventy-five years before I was born?" (p. 170).

Heilbroner claims convincingly that there is no rational answer to this question. "No argument based on reason will lead me to care for posterity or to lift a finger in its behalf" (p. 170). As evidence he quotes an unnamed professor of political economy at the University of London who wrote recently:

> → Suppose that, as a result of using up all the world's resources, human life did come to an end. So what? What is so desirable about an indefinite continuation of the human species, religious convictions apart? It may well be that nearly everybody who is already here on earth would be reluctant to die, and everybody has an instinctive fear of death. But one must not confuse this with the notion that in any meaningful sense, generations who are yet unborn can be said to be better off if they are born than if they are not.

The most interesting clause in this quotation is, of course, "religious convictions apart." It is Heilbroner's judgment that the future of the human race will depend precisely on these "religious convictions" (p. 175). His advice for survival is less convincing: "As I examine the prospect ahead, I do not only predict but prescribe a centralization of power as the only means by which our threatened and dangerous civilization will make way for its successors" (p. 165).

The only system that can turn us around is "a social order that will blend a 'religious' orientation and a 'military' discipline" (p. 161). Heilbroner calls this a "monastic organization of society," and sees it illustrated in the "socialist church" of modern China.

The question arises: is this quasi-military monasticism the only alternative to disaster or are there resources in the Christian faith which might enable us to restrain our self-destructive arrogance and pride? Heilbroner does not raise this question, but one should recall that the Christian faith enabled women and men to survive the collapse of ancient civilization and construct a new world on its ruins. It has resources to attack the very roots of our predicament so eloquently described by Heilbroner. But these resources will not be discovered by theologians who play philosophical games or church members who use faith as a means to greater self-indulgence and as a flight from reality.

G.W.F.

THE FUTURE OF THE WORLD ECONOMY. A UNITED NATIONS STUDY
by Wassily Leontief, et al. New York: Oxford University Press, 1977; 110 pp.; $4.95.

Barring war or natural catastrophe, and assuming that people will behave somewhat rationally, the next twenty years could very well be a time of real progress toward economic well-being and a greater measure of distributive justice within the world community. Such is the message of this UN commissioned report.

By way of contrast to the dire predictions of any number of best-selling Cassandras, this report is both upbeat and modest in approach. The major problems—population, food production, pollution, industrialization, and international economy relationships—confronting the world community in the next generation are (to use the report's recurring word) "manageable."

The report does not attempt to analyze political trends or to suggest how the necessary political will can be generated to bring its envisaged goals to fruition. While it counsels both saving/investment by developing countries and, at the same time, social justice in the distribution of burdens and benefits, the report does not suggest how this is to be achieved politically.

There is no discussion of the potential role of the transnational corporation. However, in view of the widespread paralysis, corruption, or incompetence of politics and politicians in relation to economic concerns, and in view of the slow emergence of transnational *public* structures, one cannot help wondering whether the TNCs will not of necessity become more and more a vehicle of such progress as is achievable. It is perhaps too much to expect such a discussion from a United Nations source inasmuch as TNCs have become part of the "New International Demonology."

The report is nevertheless valuable in that it sets forth what is "do-able" for a number of years. While some can (and should) inquire into the longer run, there is a need to know what is possible tomorrow and the day after.

R.J.N.

POPULATION AND THE AMERICAN FUTURE: THE REPORT OF THE COMMISSION ON POPULATION GROWTH AND THE AMERICAN FUTURE
New York: New American Library, 1972; 362 pp.; $1.50.

The work and report of the Commission on Population Growth and the American Future were hidden from public attention in the years from 1969 to 1972 by the more violent news of the war in Vietnam. The majority of the recommendations made by the Commission are still waiting implementation.

The sixteen chapters of the report cover every major aspect of population growth and its implications in the United States. The perspective of the Commission is not surprising: ". . . population policy goals must be sought in full consonance with the fundamental values of American life: respect for human freedom, human dignity, and individual fulfillment; and concern for social justice and social welfare." It is assumed that responsible, free action by individuals will lead cumulatively to the common good. The recommendations therefore concern voluntary legal, social, and political changes, rather than government coercion.

Some of the most far-reaching recommendations (which also elicit minority statements) concern the rights of women and education for fertility control. No less important are recommendations concerning a national land-use policy, housing and economic development for minority group persons, child care and adoption resources, and population and sex education programs.

The analysis of the effects of population growth on the economy, energy and environmental resources, and foreign policy is helpful, especially for congregational study programs.

E.A.B.

IT is a reasonable conclusion from the information presented in the preceding pages that a simple answer to the population problem eludes us partly because even the definition of the problem is so complex. One could summarize the results of the various presentations by observing: "Anyone who claims to have the answer has not understood the question."

One temptation is immediately obvious. We could despair and, out of hopelessness, try to ignore the "world's dilemma." Since we cannot see a solution we could act as if the problem did not exist. A variation on this theme is the contemplation of "fairy tale" solutions such as the resettlement of our excess population on other planets in distant solar systems. The present popularity of the so-called "space operas" may be at least partially the result of the hope that space exploration will solve the problems of an overcrowded earth, just as once-upon-a-time earth exploration solved the problems of an overcrowded Europe.

The preceding pages have outlined certain available alternatives. We could adopt one of these alternative positions in regard to the population dilemma and use all our ingenuity and power to solve the problem, on the assumption that this one particular position is the correct one and will in fact save humanity from the "Population Bomb."

(1) Freedom must be sacrificed to survival. Since "a population of more than four billion human beings cannot be sustained adequately now or in the future," vast and coercive birth control, sterilization and abortion programs are in order.

(2) The capitalist system and its technology, which created the problem, will also solve it if we only give it a chance and not hinder it by various "Luddite" schemes and "environmental impact statements," which interfere with human progress. (The capitalist exploitation of sex as entertainment and for profit will contribute further to the reduction of the birth rate since unlike rabbits, human "bunnies" are not very fertile.)

(3) A general rise in the standard of living resulting from a more equitable distribution of existing resources, goods, and services through some form of socialism, will inevitably lead to fertility declines and obviate the need for large families as means of social security. Furthermore, the liberation of women in such a system will reduce their fertility.

From a Christian perspective the last alternative (3), while operating with its share of utopian notions and false assumptions about the nature of the human predicament, seems the least offensive. Given the need for a program to confront the population crisis, the way out of the dilemma by way of a fairer distribution of the available resources seems to show the greatest promise with the smallest danger to freedom and justice. It is, however, important to avoid giving the impression that nothing can be done pending a complete change in our social system. Elements of the other solutions which have been proposed could be implemented even now.

What has to be opposed at all costs is the notion, prevalent even among writers in the field of Christian ethics, that the end justifies any means. Indeed, the magnitude of the "dilemma" tempts those aware of the dangers threatening the survival of the human race to advocate remedies so radical that they may be worse than the disease they are alleged to cure.

It is important to look carefully at the proposed medicines and make precise distinctions between those which can be tolerated and those which kill. For example, conception control measures and voluntary sterilization are vastly preferable to forced sterilization and abortion as means of population control. Similarly, family planning, while certainly not the cure-all some see in it, is a sound idea, which should, however, not result in making motherhood an "anti-value."

Especially when confronted by so complex and intricate a problem as the population explosion it is important not to lose sight of the significance of means. In choosing the wrong means, we might succeed in bringing about the continuation of the human race only to discover in the process that the erstwhile human being has become a soulless monster or a naked ape.

G.W.F.